Who Wears What?

Judith Bauer Stamper

 TeachingStrategies® · Bethesda, MD

For Teaching Strategies, LLC.
Publisher: Larry Bram
Editorial Director: Hilary Parrish Nelson
VP Curriculum and Assessment: Cate Heroman
Product Manager: Kai-leé Berke
Book Development Team: Sherrie Rudick and Jan Greenberg
Project Manager: Jo A. Wilson

For Q2AMedia
Editorial Director: Bonnie Dobkin
Editor and Curriculum Adviser: Suzanne Barchers
Program Manager: Gayatri Singh
Creative Director: Simmi Sikka
Project Manager: Santosh Vasudevan
Designers: Dalbir Singh & Ritu Chopra
Picture Researchers: Judy Brown & Stephanie Mills

Picture Credits
t-top b-bottom c-center l-left r-right

Cover: Regina Chayer/Shutterstock, Kelly Cline/Istockphoto, J Troudt/Big Stock Photo.

Back Cover: Nancy Hixson/Shutterstock.

Title page: Twobluedogs/Dreamstime.

Insides: Karen Mower/Istockphoto: 3tl, Stephen Mulcahey/ Shutterstock: 3tr, William Berry/Shutterstock: 3bl, Erasmus Wolff/ Dreamstime: 3br, Masterfile: 4t, FEMA Photolibrary: 4b, Todd Bates/ Istockphoto: 5t, NASA Human Spaceflight Collection: 5c, Remus Borisov/U.S. Navy: 5b, NASA: 6t, Mahlon K. Miller/U.S. Navy: 6b, Devon Stephens/Istockphoto: 7t, Skip O'Donnell/Istockphoto: 7c, Q2AMedia Image Bank: 7b, Emely Emely/Photolibrary: 8t, Photos. com/Jupiter Images, Eric Michaud/Istockphoto: 9t, Fotocrisis/ Shutterstock: 9b, Masterfile: 10t, Jeremy Woodhouse/Photolibrary: 10b, Shutterstock: 11tl, Istockphoto: 11tr, Lukas Pobuda/Shutterstock: 11bl, Andreea Manciu/Istockphoto: 11br, Kelly Cline/Istockphoto: 12t, Photolibrary: 12b, Nancy Hixson/Shutterstock: 13t, Mike Flippo/Shutterstock: 13b, Mike Powell/Allsport Concepts/Getty Images: 14t, J Troudt/Big Stock Photo: 14b, Lorraine Kourafas/ Shutterstock: 15r, Marco Menne/Dreamstime: 15c, Juris Popovs/ Shutterstock: 15l, Masterfile: 16t, Masterfile: 16b, Michele Cozzolino/ Dreamstime: 17r, Wendell Franks/Istockphoto: 17c, Microstocker/ Shutterstock: 17b, Photos.com/Jupiterimages: 18t, Istockphoto: 18b, Angelika Schwarz/Istockphoto: 19t, Istockphoto: 19c, Dreamstime: 19bl, Istockphoto: 19br, Regina Chayer/Shutterstock: 20t, Istockphoto: 20b, Lisa Thornberg/Istockphoto: 21tl, Emin Ozkan/ Shutterstock: 21tr, Lepas/Shutterstock: 21bl, Ironi/Shutterstock: 21br, Ariel Skelley/Photolibrary: 22t, Jennifer Russell/Dreamstime: 22b, Masterfile: 23t, Comstock/Jupiterimages: 23b, Varina and Jay Patel/ Shutterstock: 24.

Teaching Strategies, LLC.
Bethesda, MD
www.TeachingStrategies.com

ISBN: 978-1-60617-120-2

Library of Congress Cataloging-in-Publication Data
Stamper, Judith Bauer.
    Who wears what? / Judith Bauer Stamper.
        p. cm.
    ISBN 978-1-60617-120-2
    1. Clothing and dress--Juvenile literature. I. Title.
    GT518.S69 2010
    391--dc22
                        2009044305

CPSIA tracking label information:
RR Donnelley, Shenzhen, China
Date of Production: Jan 2017
Cohort: Batch 6

Printed and bound in China

8 9 10	17
Printing	Year Printed

Who wears what?

Guess who!

Police Officer

I wear my uniform and a holster when I am on the job. I'm proud to wear my badge, too. It tells everyone that I am dedicated to keeping people safe.

Firefighter

When there's a fire or an emergency, I come to the rescue! My helmet protects my head and neck from heat and sparks. My jacket and pants are made of special cloth that won't burn or melt.

Who wears what?

Guess who!

Astronaut

My space suit protects me when I am traveling in the space shuttle or working in outer space. It gives me air to breathe and keeps me warm.

Navy Shooter

I help launch planes from Navy aircraft carriers. Pilots can easily see the bright colors of my clothes. My earphones block out noise from those very loud jet engines.

Who wears what?

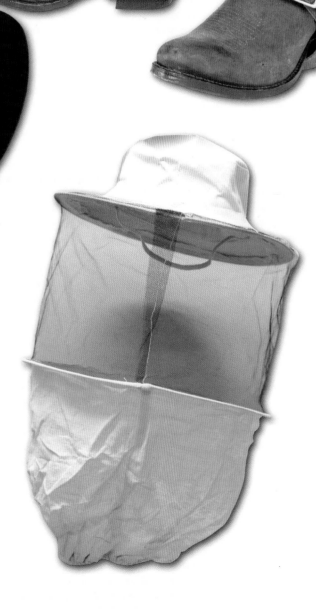

Guess who!

We do!
We wear special clothes
when we work outdoors
with animals.

Cowboy

You can usually find me riding the range on my horse. My boots protect my ankles from the stirrups. My hat keeps me cool in the hot sun. My rugged jeans are tough enough for the hard work I do.

Beekeeper

My bees seldom sting me, but I still wear a special bee suit to protect myself. A veil protects my face, and gloves cover my hands as I work.

Who wears what?

Guess who!

**We do!
We love to perform
in front of audiences.**

Ballet Dancer

I wear beautiful costumes like this pink tutu as I twirl across the stage. I couldn't dance on my toes like this if my pointed shoes didn't have stiff tips.

Mariachi Band

People clap and cheer when we play our mariachi music. We wear wide-brimmed hats with silver-studded jackets and pants.

Who wears what?

Guess who!

**We do!
Our work puts food
on your table.**

Chef

I am a chef, and my big white hat is called a toque. I also wear a crisp white jacket as I prepare each delicious meal.

Fisherman

I catch fish from a fishing boat. My rubber boots keep me from slipping on the wet deck. My orange slicker and my hat protect me from the wind and waves.

Who wears what?

Guess who!

Soccer Player

I'm proud to wear my team jersey. My shin guards and socks protect my legs. My cleats dig into the ground as I kick the ball.

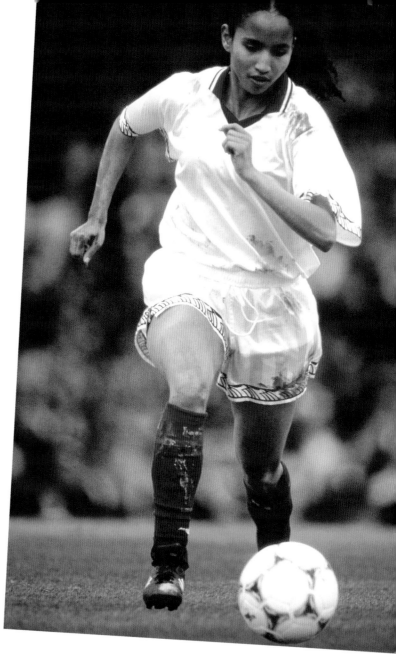

Baseball Catcher

I use my leather mitt to catch the balls that speed past the batter. My face guard and chest protector protect me from the balls I miss!

Who wears what?

Guess who!

Dentist

I wear gloves and a mask as protection from germs. If you have a cavity or a broken tooth, don't worry! I'll keep your teeth healthy and your smile bright.

Doctor

I keep a prescription pad in my pocket and a stethoscope around my neck. I listen to your heart and lungs, and then I check your eyes and ears. I try to make sure you stay healthy, but I'll take care of you when you're not.

Who wears what?

Guess who!

> **We do!**
> **We fix things that are broken, from cars to light switches.**

Mechanic

Our coveralls keep us from getting covered in grease and dirt. They also help protect our skin from dangerous chemicals as we work on car batteries and electrical systems.

Handyman

Do you need something fixed? In my tool belt and tool box, I carry the right tool for every job. My hard hat protects me from falling objects.

Who wears what?

Guess who!

Clown

People laugh when they see me coming down the street. I wear a silly wig, a baggy suit, and colorful shoes.

Mime

I wear a black hat, a white shirt, and paint on my face. I am a mime, and I tell stories without saying a word.

Who wears what?

Guess who!

You do!

You wear special clothes when it's hot and when it's cold. You wear different outfits for sports and for celebrations.

Hot

Cold

Sports

Party

What will you wear today?